This Book Belongs to:

Annette and Her Pet:
A Story of Love and Loss

Written By **Felicia C. Lucas** Illustrated By **Sanghamitra Dasgupta**

Text Copyright © 2023 Felicia C. Lucas

Illustration Copyright © 2023 Sanghamitra Dasgupta

All rights reserved

ISBN: 978-1-950861-81-1

Thank you for purchasing this book and complying with copyright laws by not reproducing, scanning, or distributing any part of it in any form without permission.

Published by His Glory Creations Publishing, LLC

Wendell, North Carolina

Printed in the United States

About the Book

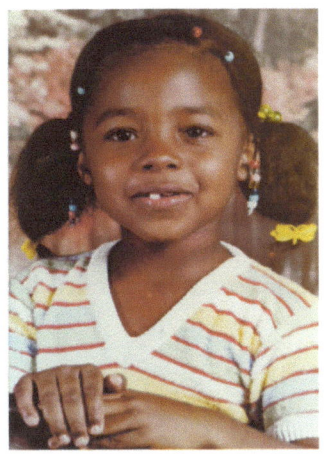

Author Felicia "Annette" at an early age

Based on the author's true experience of losing her first pet, Carrie, this book was written for younger children who have experienced the death of their bird, hamster, puppy, kitten, or other pet.

Children are encouraged to understand that sadness is a step in the process of healing. Adults sometimes don't recognize that children go through the stages of grief when they lose their pet just like when adults grieve the loss of loved ones.

Pets are more than just animals; they are often a part of the family unit. It is natural for parents to desire to protect their children from the painful experience of grief. With proper support, a child can process the loss and heal overtime.

Parents, grandparents, guardians, teachers, or gift givers can use this book as a conversational piece to assist a child through their grief process.

Five-year-old Annette loved her pet bird, Carrie, a beautiful green and yellow parakeet. Carrie lived in a bird cage in the family room.

Annette loved to rub Carrie's smooth feathers and enjoyed feeding her bird seeds.

Every day, Annette let Carrie out of the cage to fly around in the house.

Sometimes she would open the back door so Carrie could fly outside. Carrie would go outside for a little while but would always return home.

One day, when Annette let Carrie out of the cage, Carrie flew straight into the closed backdoor, and there was a loud thump.

Annette didn't understand what was happening to Carrie. Her dad explained that Carrie had a bad accident and was no longer with them.

Annette was so sad that Carrie was gone. She began to cry and miss her pet bird.

She helped bury Carrie in the backyard, in a special place, right next to the back door. At an early age, Annette learned about losing a pet.

As time passed, Annette wasn't crying as much and continued to remember all the fun times she had with Carrie.

Even though she missed Carrie, Annette was filled with joy when she received a special gift, her new puppy, Rex. This was the beginning of a new friendship.

RESOURCES FOR PARENTS AND CHILDREN

ALL ABOUT MY PET

Picture of my Pet

One of the most difficult parts about losing a pet may be sharing the news to kids. Talk to them in a place where they feel safe and comfortable and not easily distracted.

If your pet is very old or has a long illness, consider talking to kids before the death happens.

If you had to euthanize your pet, you may want to explain that:

- The veterinarian did everything that they could do

- This was the kindest way to take the pet's pain away

- Their pet died peacefully, without feeling hurt or scared

It is important for children to have the opportunity to say goodbye to their pet. This can be as a ceremony or even a part of the burying process.

Children should always have choices as to how much they wish to be involved with saying goodbye.

Be prepared to explain several times about what happened since they will often continue to ask where their pet is and when it will come back.

It is best to describe their pet's death saying that the pet has stopped moving, does not see or hear anymore, and will not wake up.

You may hear, "Why did my pet have to die?" and "Will I ever see my pet again?" With every question, be honest with your answer.

Encourage your child to talk openly about death so that you can understand it from their point of view and can provide proper support and encouragement through the process.

Questions to ask a child concerning their pet:

1. What did you love most about your pet?

2. What do you miss about your pet?

3. What are some of your favorite memories with your pet?

About the Author

Felicia "Annette" Clemons Lucas is an International Best-Selling author with 22 literary projects that she has authored, co-authored, or compiled.

She is a wife, mother of 3, licensed minister, speaker, non-profit co-founder, certified health/life coach, and an award-winning publisher.

In 2017, she became the Founder/CEO of His Glory Creations Publishing, LLC, an international Christian Publishing Company, after releasing her first book, Make it Happen: Moving Towards Your Best U.

Felicia is a graduate of the University of North Carolina at Chapel Hill where she obtained a Bachelor of Arts Degree in Communications. She also has over 25 years of experience in the Human Resources Field.

When she is not writing and/or publishing books for others, Felicia loves to travel, watches Hallmark movies and spends time with her family.

Contact Felicia today at www.felicialucas.com

His Glory Creations Publishing, LLC is an International Christian Book Publishing Company, established in 2017, which helps launch the creative works of new, aspiring, and seasoned authors across the globe, through stories that are inspirational, empowering, life changing or educational in nature, including fiction, non-fiction, memoirs, anthologies, poetry books, journals, children's books, and audio books.

DESIRE TO KNOW MORE?

Contact Information:
CEO/Founder: Felicia C. Lucas
www.hisglorycreationspublishing.com
Email: hgcpublishingllc@gmail.com
Office Phone: 919-679-1706
Facebook: His Glory Creations Publishing
Instagram: His Glory Creations Publishing
YouTube: His Glory Creations Publishing

www.ingramcontent.com/pod-product-compliance
Lightning Source LLC
Chambersburg PA
CBHW050752110526
44592CB00002B/35